A SIMPLY WONDERFUL LIFE

A Guide to Easy Organization

By Dee Armstrong Crabtree

Second Edition

ABOUT THE AUTHOR

Dee Armstrong Crabtree is a freelance author and a professional organizer. An Indiana native, she is the mother of two and the grandmother of two. She studied Journalism at Indiana's Saint Mary-of-the-Woods College and has been published in several local, regional and national publications.

COPYRIGHT INFORMATION

Copyright 2007, Dee Armstrong Crabtree, all rights. The lists contained in Chapter XXII are not copyrighted and copying of those pages is permitted.

Published by Dee Armstrong Crabtree
ISBN 978-0-6151-6741-1

ALSO BY THE SAME AUTHOR

A, Simply Wonderful Holiday, A Holiday Guide and Planner for 2007

DEDICATION

This small book is dedicated to the memory of my precious grandmother, Regency Perkins, whose own home was a wonderful sanctuary full of undying love and precious memories.

It is my hope that the tips contained in this little book will help you create that same kind of sanctuary in your home and that you will live a simply wonderful life.

A NOTE FROM THE AUTHOR

I hope you enjoy this book and find the information here useful. This book will be expanded and improved upon year after year. This is the second edition.

Please be sure to visit my website at http://organizerdee.tripod.com or drop me an email at organizerdee@yahoo.com. I'd love to hear your questions about organizing, as well as your feedback on the book. When you do write, please be sure to sign up for my free monthly email newsletter.

The hints contained in these pages are presented to you in hopes of helping you make your life easier and more enjoyable. Following these guidelines will not lead to more work for you but will actually save you time, energy and money.

Organizing your home can be a fun, creative and satisfying undertaking if you approach it with the right attitude. Try to relax and enjoy the process of taking control of your belongings, your time and your life.

CONTENTS

I. In The Beginning
II. Tackling Time
III. Managing Any Mess
IV. Bargain Organizing Tools
V. Quicker Cleaning
VI. Bathrooms
VII. Kitchens
VIII. Family Rooms
IX. Bedrooms
X. Children's Rooms
XI. Guest Rooms
XII. Closets
XIII. Garages
XIV. Cars
XV. Laundry
XVI. Grocery Shopping
XVII. Paperwork & Computer Files
XVIII. Travel
XIX. Holidays
XX. Entertaining
XXI. Household Moves
XXII. Lists
    a. Grocery Shopping
    b. Holiday Gift List
    c. Christmas Card Register
    d. Travel Packing List
    e. Before Leaving Home
    f. Helpful Websites

CHAPTER I

IN THE BEGINNING

A thoroughly organized life is a simply wonderful life. Imagine how stress-free your life would be if you never again had to search for misplaced bills, keys or homework. Imagine how blissful it would be to instantly put your fingers on everything you need anytime you need it.

This book is your guide to quick, easy and inexpensive organization in your life. None of the tips or tools detailed here will cost you much time or money. Most of the tools we talk about here are items you probably already have sitting around your house.

Organizing your home can feel overwhelming in the beginning. Just relax and take it slow and easy. As the old saying goes, Rome wasn't built in a day – and you sure couldn't clean it in a day! Chances are that your mess didn't grow overnight so you shouldn't expect to clean it up overnight either.

Before you can organize a space, you need to find the time to do it. Start with the "Tackling Time" chapter and learn how to carve a little more time into your schedule. Next pick the area of your home that bothers you the most, whether it is your bathroom cabinet, your kitchen pantry or your desk. This book is categorized by area, so pick your first project and flip to the corresponding chapter to begin.

When you begin, think outside the box – literally! Be as creative as you can be. A little creativity can save you a whole lot of space, time and money. For example, you don't have to store that artificial Christmas tree in the cumbersome box it came in. Brainstorm all of the possible alternative solutions. Can you store it in a clean lidded trash can in the garage? Can you disassemble it and store it in a couple of boxes under your bed? Could you hang it from bike hooks attached to the rafters in your garage or basement? When you use a little creativity, you can greatly increase your storage and organization options.

Be a rebel and break all the traditional rules of organization. You don't have to follow those old rules if they don't suit your lifestyle. Put things where you use them most. If you don't usually come in through your front door, why hang your coats in the front closet? Wouldn't a closet or coat rack by the back door make more sense? Most people keep their shoes in their bedroom closets. However, if you like to take off your shoes the minute you get home, keep everyday shoes in a shoe bag that hangs over the door closest to where you come in at the end of the day. Likewise, if you always take the dog outside through the kitchen door, keep the leash in a basket or on a hook placed near that door.

Try to have fun with your organizing projects. Enjoy the creative side of organizing. The point of organizing is not to try to conform to someone else's idea of how your home should be, but rather to create a home where you can live in comfort and ease. Don't fall into the trap of thinking that your closets should look like the pictures you see in magazines. Concentrate on making your life easier, not impressing others with your organizing projects.

Take pride in your home organizing accomplishments. Being organized can free up time in your schedule to do all the things you've often dreamt of doing. Too often we make plans and then put them off because we can't find the tools and materials we need. Once you become organized, you won't have to put off those special plans any longer.

Organizing your home gives you the opportunity to share your blessings with others. Consider passing the things you no longer need or want to needy family members or to charities in your community. If you have too many pots and pans, hand them down to your newly-wedded niece. Send clothing you no longer use to the battered women's shelter. There are countless worthy organizations in your community that could find great value in the things collecting dust in your home.

At the back of this book you will find some basic lists that will help you simplify your everyday life. Please feel free to take this book to a copy machine and make as many copies of those lists you as need.

Your life will be so much simpler and so much more enjoyable if you organize your time and your home to suit your needs and your lifestyle. Take a few moments to think about how you live your life and about what small changes you can implement that will make your life easier and better. Flip through this book at your leisure and pick out all of the best ideas that will help you in your quest to make your life simply wonderful.

CHAPTER II

TACKLING TIME

If you intend to organize your home, you're probably wondering how you will ever find the time to do it, so let's start with some simple timesaving tips.

Keep your everyday wardrobe simple. Limit yourself to one purse for daily use. There will be special occasions when you will want to carry another style, but your life will be much easier if you stick to using the same purse day after day. If you pick one with several pockets and dividers built in, and you use those pockets consistently, you will always know where your cash, bank card, nail files and lipstick are.

Consider sticking to one daily set of jewelry also. If you stick to plain gold or silver, you'll be able to wear the same earrings, rings, necklaces and bracelets everyday. You want to look nice every day but there really is no rule that says you have to look remarkably different every day.

You need on ever present organizing tool, something to track your appointments, to do lists, grocery lists, etc. You may use a PDA or expensive organizer to keep track of the details of your life but if those tools seem a little bulky or inconvenient for you, consider an inexpensive spiral notebook instead. You can buy three little notepads for about $1.00. Use them to jot down phone numbers, grocery lists and to do lists.

Try to consolidate your errands in order to save time and money. Many of us tend to run our regular errands on Saturday, but if you live out in the suburbs, away from a commercial area, it might make more sense for you to run those errands on your way home from work during the week.

Think about how often you are in one room and you have to go to another room to get scissors, an ink pen or a tissue. You'll save yourself an amazing amount of time running around the house fetching everyday items if you keep these little things in every room in your home: Scissors, ink pens, a trash can, tape, a clock and tissues.

Don't try to do everything yourself. Even Martha Stewart is known to have hired household help. Enlist your kids, grandkids and spouses to help. They might not do things exactly the way you would, but they can help you get things done. It doesn't really matter if the towels are folded and stacked just right, just as long as they are close to the tub when you need them. If you don't have kids of your own, hire some neighborhood kids. They can walk the dog, carry boxes up and down stairs, water plants, pull weeds and do countless other small household chores.

Do you feel like you have too many demands on your time to exercise? Combine exercise with your social time by walking with your friends and neighbors. If you have a dog that you spend time petting and playing with every evening, try getting him out for a long walk instead.

Keep a workout bag with spare sneakers and/or workout gear in the car so that you can take advantage of unexpected pockets of time to work out. If a friend is late meeting you for lunch, you can change into those sneakers and take a quick walk while you wait.

The Internet is a wonderful organizational tool. You can save time and money by checking out the best prices in town for almost anything you want to buy. In addition, most of the major retailers offer home delivery of your purchases. You can have clothing, books, music, computers, furniture, groceries and just about anything else you want delivered to your home when you shop on-line.

Many people spend a lot of time on emails. If you find yourself wasting time on the computer, try to limit checking your email to once a day. Don't feel like you have to be in constant contact with your family and friends, answering each and every email immediately upon its arrival.

Some experts recommend putting the things you need to take with you in the morning by the door where you'll see them in the morning. When I'm in a morning fog, I can still walk right past those things and forget to take them along. I've learned to put the things I need to take with me in the morning directly into car the night before.

Although many shampoos instruct you to lather, rinse & repeat, try shampooing your hair just once in the morning. Many high quality shampoos actually recommend the once over instead of the traditional two soapings, saving you both time and money.

To drastically cut blow drying time, blot your hair with paper towels just before you apply your styling products.

If mornings are hectic for you, try to do as many grooming chores as you can in the evening, such as shaving your legs, plucking your eyebrows, etc. Likewise, lay out all of your clothing and accessories the night before.

Try to eliminate scheduling unnecessary chores for the morning. You can feed the dog, do the dishes and sign school papers in the evening instead of in the morning.

Set up your coffee maker and set out your breakfast dishes at night before you go to bed. If you always drink coffee on your way to work, set your travel mug next to the coffee maker when you take it out of the dishwasher in the evening.

What do you spend the most time looking for? Most people misplace their keys on a daily basis. The key (pardon the pun), is to always put your keys in the same place. At home, put a key rack by the door and hang your keys there the moment you walk in the door. When you're out running errands, always put your keys in the same place in your purse or in the same pocket. If you are consistent about where you put your keys, you will never have to look for them again.

CHAPTER III

MANAGING ANY MESS

The process for cleaning up virtually any mess is the same. Consider this process as the basic project management format for any space you want to organize, be it a drawer, a closet or a room.

STEP ONE

Clear the area. You cannot effectively organize anything until you have a clear workspace. Move everything out of the closet, cabinet or room that you want to organize.

STEP TWO

Divide everything you remove into three piles.

The Keep it Pile – This pile should only contain the things that you truly care about or that are useful to your current lifestyle. Your storage space is valuable "real estate" and things that have no use or are meaningless to you is a waste of that valuable real estate.

The Pitch it Pile – Everything has an expiration date, no matter how sentimental you may feel about it. Throw away anything that is broken beyond repair or worn out. Throw away duplicate or unflattering pictures. You may have been conditioned to keep spare items "just in case." However, consider that the space you gain may be much more valuable to you than that extra toaster or those old worn out sweaters.

The Pass it on Pile – You may own some things that are still useful but that just are not useful to you. You can sell the items in this stack, but I highly suggest you donate the items to charity. If you donate to charity and obtain a tax receipt from the organization you donated to, the tax deduction that you earn from that donation may actually be worth more to you than the cash you receive from selling those items. Many charities will welcome your used but still usable clothing, dishes, decorations, appliances, office equipment and even cars.

STEP THREE

Organize what is left. The final step is to put the things in your "Keep It" pile neatly back into your space. Find appropriate containers for what is left. If you need to buy new containers, be sure to measure your storage space before you buy so that you know what size of containers to get to fit into your space. You don't want to clutter your space with useless containers.

CHAPTER IV

BARGAIN ORGANIZING TOOLS

There are many wonderful, sophisticated organizing systems that you can invest in to improve your home. Keep in mind that you don't have to spend a lot of money to effectively organize your space. You can save the earth and save some of your hard earned money at the same time if you recycle everyday household items. Recycled copy paper boxes, shoe boxes, baskets and decorative plastic bins all serve very well as cost-efficient storage.

Copy Paper Boxes – You can store nearly everything in these boxes! They can be used to store decorations, tools, toys, clothes, etc. Their uniform shape and size make them stack well. Use a large permanent marker to mark the end of the box with the contents.

Shoeboxes – Use shoeboxes as dividers in any cabinet, closet or drawer.

Cup Hooks – Cup hooks come in all sizes and they hold so much more than cups. You can use them to hold keys, belts, kitchen utensils and jewelry.

Nails & Screws – Fill the walls or studs of your garage with sturdy nails and screws and hang your brooms, shovels and other tools in this otherwise wasted space.

Tissue Boxes – Wad up those plastic bags from the grocery store, stuff them in an empty tissue box and then pull them out as the need arises.

Mugs – Mugs can corral pens, cosmetics, medicines, paint tubes, crochet needles, manicure implements, paperclips and spare change.

Junk Mail Envelopes – Stash some in your purse and car to use as notepaper.

Paper Towel Cardboard – Fold extension cords and slide them inside the paper towel roller.

Baskets & Bowls – Decorate your home with attractive baskets and bowls and you'll have plenty of storage for small items. Baskets on top of your cabinets can store your out-of-season items or seldom used cooking utensils.

Stationery Boxes – Use an empty stationery box for an in-box on your desk or next to your printer to hold extra printer paper.

Plastic Bins – Plastic bins go on sale in almost every discount store during the month of January. They provide excellent waterproof, airtight storage.

Lidded Trash Cans – While most people don't think of using trash cans for storage, a clean lidded trash can provides storage for large otherwise difficult to store items such as sports equipment or holiday decorations.

Canning Jars – All of our grandmothers used these for years and they used them for much more than canning food. Store buttons, matches, marbles, spare change, pet treats and countless other collections of small items in these charming containers.

Suitcases – Suitcases can take up a lot of room in your closet so don't store them empty. Use them to hold your linens, purses and other smaller suitcases.

Car Trunk – You normally don't want to carry a lot of extra weight in the trunk of your car, but there may come a time when company is coming and you need to get the golf bags out of the entryway closet to make room for your guests' things. You can store those golf clubs and a lot of other things in the trunk of your car for the duration of the visit.

Egg Cartons – You can store jewelry neatly and safely in egg cartons. They're also great to hold small craft supplies and hardware.

If you do need to buy organizing supplies the best places to buy them are home improvement stores, discount stores and office supply stores. Office supply stores often offer the most affordable and innovative organizing solutions.

CHAPTER V

QUICKER CLEANING

Always work from top to bottom when cleaning. Dust and clean the mirrors before you vacuum.

Work clockwise around the room in order to keep your forward momentum going and to cut down on walking back and forth across the room.

Avoid confusing cleaning chores with fix-up or redecorating projects. Try to concentrate solely on cleaning and then go back at another time to repair or redecorate.

Before using chemical cleaners on fabric or carpet stains, first try using a slightly damp, nubby washcloth on the spot. Many fabrics have stain resistant qualities and will come clean with just the smallest bit of rubbing on the spot.

To soak up spills on carpet, first blot the spill with a paper towel. Then cover the entire spot with table salt and then let it sit for 24 hours before you vacuum it up. This treatment will remove most stains, but you may need to follow up with a spray on stain remover for more stubborn stains.

If you live in a two-story home, keep a complete set of cleaning supplies, including vacuum cleaners, on both floors.

Keep a toilet brush and cleaner in each bathroom of the house so you don't have to lug them back and forth between the different rooms.

Use lint rollers for quick removal of pet hair from the sofa. To cut down on the pet hair that actually lands on the sofa, brush your pet and then gently roll the roller directly over him/her.

Consider not making your bed on a daily basis. Does anyone see it while you're at work all day? Do you see it any time during the day?

Use the new electromagnetic "feather" dusters and you'll not only save time but your manicure as well.

You can drastically cut down on dusting time if you change your furnace filter once a month.

Put doormats both inside and outside all of your entry doors to cut down on dirt tracked into the house.

Straighten every room daily to prevent clutter buildup.

Set a timer while you clean. Determine how much time you want to spend in each room. Working with the timer running will keep you focused and moving forward.

Keep a basket or box on each floor for items that should be moved to the other floor. As you clean, drop items in this box and then tote it up or down when you're done cleaning that floor.

Sounds simple, but don't clean what isn't dirty. Do you really need to dust the side of the entertainment center? Scrub a sink that hasn't been used all week?

Top your refrigerator with a layer of clear wrap. When it gets dirty, simply peel it off and replace it with a clean sheet of wrap.

Oh no! You just got a call that Aunt Bertha is coming to visit and she's only ten minutes away. The house is a mess. What will you do? Here's your battle plan:

- Pick up a laundry basket and then run around the public areas of the house picking up newspapers, mail, toys and anything else that will fit into the basket. Stash the basket in a closet or pantry until your guest leaves.

- Grab the window cleaner and some paper towels. Do a quick swipe of any mirrors or shiny surfaces your guest will see. Do a quick swipe of the powder room and kitchen sinks also and hang fresh hand towels nearby.

- Empty the powder room trash can and any other trash cans your guest will see.

- Close the doors to any rooms that you don't want your visitor going into.

- Put dirty dishes in the dishwasher. If you don't have a dishwasher, rinse the dirty dishes, put them into roasting pan and hide them in the oven. (Yes, the oven. Just don't forget to take them out right after your visitor leaves.)
- Lower the lights. If it's daylight, adjust the blinds so not too much sunlight comes in.
- Run the vacuum quickly across the main areas of the carpet.
- Spray air freshener or light a candle for a little nicer atmosphere.

The best way to keep household clutter under control is to do a one-minute "run-through" in every room every day. Once a day, preferably just before bedtime, spend just one minute in each room straightening it up. One minute a day. Even if you live in a ten room house, that's only ten minutes a day.

CHAPTER VI

BATHROOMS

We all begin and end our days in the bathroom. Organizing your bathroom is a small effort but the payoffs are huge. Try a few of these tricks.

Hooks are lifesavers in any bathroom. Put robe hooks on the back of all your bathroom doors, including the guest bathroom.

Hooks in the linen closet can hold your bath tray and your hairdryer. If your bathroom lacks a linen closet, those same hooks can be installed inside the vanity doors.

Installing racks inside the vanity doors can nearly double your storage space.

Keep a full set of cleaning supplies in each bathroom to save time running back and forth for the things you need when cleaning.

Paper towels in the bath also come in handy for quick mirror or sink cleaning. Install a paper towel holder just inside a bathroom cabinet.

Set a hamper or basket just for towels in each bathroom. When full, pick up the basket and dump it into the washing machine – no sorting required!

You most likely use the same products every day for your skin and hair care routines. You'll save time if you put those daily use products in one basket or bin for easy access. Storing your special occasion items elsewhere will help eliminate daily digging through unnecessary items. Plastic carriers designed to be used for housecleaning are especially good for this.

If space allows, give each member their own drawer in the bathroom, making it off limits to everyone else. If you don't have enough drawers to do that, give each household member their own basket for grooming essentials, bath toys, bubble bath, etc. Each person can store their bath basket in their bedroom and take it with them at bath time.

Use a mesh bag to store tub toys. Hang it from the tub faucet to let the toys drain and dry.

Store the roll of trash bags in the bottom of the trash can under the bag currently being used and you won't have to go searching for replacements every time you empty the trash.

Store your bath poufs in a basket next to tub. It not only looks pretty but the poufs always be within easy reach when you need them.

No one ever uses toilet paper in the hallway, so why store it in the hallway closet? Stash your extra rolls of toilet paper in the bathrooms, not in the hallway linen cabinets.

CHAPTER VII

KITCHENS

The kitchen is the universal heart of the home. In addition to being a food preparation area, the kitchen often serves as a communication center, homework area, a project room, a gathering place, dining room and sometimes a laundry room. That's an awful lot going on in one room and, as a result, kitchen is often the most disorganized room in the house. The kitchen will be your biggest organizing challenge.

Leave love notes, instructions and phone messages on a kitchen blackboard. Be sure to use one that has a chalk tray attached.

Create your own recipe book with a three-ring binder and clear protector pockets. You can slip entire magazine pages or photocopied recipes into those pockets. If you happen to spill something on the pages, they wipe clean.

Every kitchen should have a plastic grocery bag dispenser. Your dispenser may be as simple as an old tissue box or you could invest $4.00 or $5.00 in a plastic dispenser that mounts inside a cabinet door.

Use baskets in your pantry to organize pastas, spices, popcorn and other small packages that often get scattered and lost among larger items.

Save on cabinet storage by storing your beer mugs in the freezer, where they'll always be handy for frosty drinks.

Consider using display items such as decorative boxes and baskets for extra storage, particularly on top of your cabinets and your refrigerator.

Store your large serving platters and extra table linens in one or two big baskets on top of your fridge.

Store coffee filters in a small round basket near your coffee maker.

If you established your household some time ago, you probably have extra pots and pans that you don't need or want.

Donate them to a local charity or pass them on to needy newlyweds in your own family.

Reuse those plastic butter tubs. Use them to take cookies to the neighbors or send leftovers home with visitors.

Store leftovers in plastic butter tubs and if they happen to stay in the refrigerator long enough to resemble science experiments, you can simply throw them away without guilt.

Rolling kitchen islands come in handy, particularly when entertaining. If you don't have the floor space in your kitchen for one, consider removing the bottom shelf of your pantry so that a cart can slide neatly into that space when you're not using it. When entertaining, you can use the cart as an extra work surface while preparing the meal and then cover it with a nice tablecloth during the party for extra serving space for deserts or drinks.

Tall trays and large frying pans often create storage problems. Place a file stacker from the office supply store into a lower cabinet to neatly line up your cutting boards, cookie sheets and frying pans.

Another wonderful space saver is a stemware rack that mounts underneath your kitchen cabinets. You can also purchase cookbook racks that install underneath the cabinet and hold your cookbook open while you work.

Several kitchen utensils can hang on cup hooks under your cabinets. Hang your can opener, vegetable peeler or metal measuring cups on a magnetic strip attached anywhere near your central workspace.

Your kitchen may have little pockets of hidden space you haven't noticed. You can hang racks on the backs of your pantry door or entry door.

Home improvement stores sell a variety of small, decorative shelf kits that you can easily install at the end of your kitchen cabinets or in small corners by the doors.

Slide a folding stepstool in the small space between the fridge and the wall.

Use turntables for spices and canned goods inside your cabinets.

Use extra baking dishes to hold your spices and other small items in the pantry.

Hanging pot racks are excellent space savers. If you choose one with a grid or solid top, you can also place the pot lids on top of the rack.

If you have beautiful dishes that take up entirely too much cabinet space, consider using them to decorate your kitchen. Hang the plates on a wall, put teapots to use as countertop canisters and use extra serving bowls filled with fruit as centerpieces.

Look for wasted space underneath cabinets and next to appliances. A small dog can crate can slide neatly into the knee space of an area that was designed to work as a kitchen desk.

Use spring-type clothespins to close bags of chips rather than spending money on special clips.

Coffee filters do more than keep the grounds out of your coffee. You can lay one out on your counter for a disposable spoon rest or hand them out to kids to use as popcorn bowls.

If you have a recipe that calls for a small amount of chopped onion, chop the whole thing and put the remainder in a sealed plastic bag in the fridge or the freezer for future use in another recipe.

Freeze leftover vegetables to use later when making stews.

Freeze whole brown bananas, peel and all. When you're ready to make a banana cake, simply defrost and mash.

You'll never have to search for your kitchen timer if you buy a magnetic one that sticks on the side of your fridge or on your range hood.

Use a decorative plant stand to hold baskets or bowls of potatoes, onions and fruit.

Store ultra-sharp items, such as apple slicers and potato peelers, in thick plastic bags to avoid cut fingers.

Clean out the fridge every week on the day before trash day in order to avoid growing science experiments in the back of the fridge.

No room in the fridge to thaw that turkey? Thaw it outdoors in a cooler placed on your back porch or in your unheated garage.

Got pretty plates that are a bit chipped around the edges? Line them up on top of your cabinets for a pretty wallpaper border effect. The tiny chips won't show up at that distance.

Use a low bookcase instead of sideboard in your dining area. Use it to display your nice serving dishes. During a large dinner, it can become an extra serving area for drinks or desserts.

Paint an entertainment center to match your kitchen and use it to house your microwave, cookbook collection and pottery.

If you have trouble opening a jar, put your rubber dishwashing gloves on to allow you to get a better grip. If you don't have rubber gloves, try wrapping a large rubber band around the lid. (A rubber band works especially well for difficult nail polish bottles.)

CHAPTER VIII

FAMILY ROOMS

Look for furniture that serves double duty. A large storage ottoman or a coffee table with large drawers can hold games, movies, photo albums and afghans.

Repurpose your unused firewood stacker for newspapers bound for the recycling bin.

Look for storage behind and beneath your sofa and loveseat. Slide folding chairs, table leaves and boxed board games in these usually wasted spaces.

If book storage is an issue, consider creating risers for your table lamps and pottery by stacking attractive hardbound books together.

If you have antique books that you would like displayed but not handled, mount them in shadow boxes where they can be seen but not disturbed.

Use a decorative vase to display your fireplace matches.

If pet hair is a daily problem, instead of vacuuming the sofa every day, keep a lint roller handy and roll it over the messy areas to do a quick pickup.

Use the ashes from your wood burning stove or fireplace to fertilize your garden.

Store your remote controls in baskets or decorative boxes.

CHAPTER IX

BEDROOMS

Storing things under the bed is not a new concept. However, your options for using that space have changed. Not only can you find inexpensive cardboard boxes that will slide neatly into that space, but you can also buy wheeled carts that roll underneath the bed. If your bed sits too low to put things under it, look for inexpensive bed risers from the bed and bath store. These risers fit under each leg of your bed and can raise it six to ten inches to create the height you need for a substantial amount of extra storage. You use this space to store linens, clothing, holiday decorations, card tables, folding chairs, table leaves and more.

Store your linens at the foot of your bed in a cedar chest or storage bench.

Store your pajamas in small chests of drawers that double as nightstands.

If you don't want or have a dresser in your bedroom, stack plastic storage drawers high in a walk-in closet. Use separate drawers for different categories of clothing. Try one for light colored under things, another for darks. These drawers are often on sale for as little as $5.00 to $10.00 each, depending on the size of the drawer. You can add as many as you need over time and arrange them to fit your space.

You can hide several items beneath a skirted table round, particularly if you stack hatboxes underneath the table.

Stack antique suitcases by your bed to create unique nightstands that can also hold your extra linens and out of season items.

Don't you just hate folding fitted sheets? Just don't do it. When you launder your sheets, take them straight from the dryer and just put the same set back on the bed. You'll never have to fold sheets again if you use this method for every bed in the house.

CHAPTER X

CHILDREN'S ROOMS

Paint one wall or section of a wall with blackboard paint so that the kids can create artwork whenever they want. Buy multi-colored chalk and encourage them to change their designs to celebrate the current holidays.

Kids very rarely line things up neatly on shelves. Using baskets and pins that they can just toss toys into will make clean-up a breeze, even for a toddler.

Buy sturdy under the bed boxes for the toys your kids play with most. Most kids wind up playing on the floor by their bed anyway and having a bin right there handy will speed bedtime cleanup.

Do an annual cleanout of the kids' toys just before Christmas. Most kids are a little more willing to give up their old toys when they are excited about making room for the new ones Santa will soon be bringing. Donate outgrown toys that are still in good condition to charity.

Most kids love to play dress-up, particularly with hand-me-down evening wear. Got a satin bridesmaid dress, a feather boa, white gloves or over-sized straw hats? You might not ever want to wear them in public again but your children or grandchildren will have a ball dressing up in them. The shinier or glitzier the clothes are, the more the kids will love them. You can keep them in a trunk or a basket set aside just for those dress-up clothes. A big mirror in the play area completes the setting for an entire afternoon of old-fashioned fun.

If you have step-children or grandchildren who visit often, keep a toothbrush, pajamas and change of clothing on hand for each child and you will never have to worry about what they might have forgotten while they were packing.

Old adult-sized t-shirts and sweatshirts are great stand-ins for forgotten pajamas for little ones.

CHAPTER XI

GUEST ROOMS

Save the hotel shampoo bottles and soaps that you bring home from your next trip and put them in baskets in the guest bath.

Put a nightlight somewhere in the bedroom or put a flashlight next to the bed.

A carafe of cool water and a drinking glass on the nightstand will save your guests from having to get up and stumble around in a strange dark house in the middle of the night.

Put a fresh set of towels for your guests at the foot of the bed so that they don't have to guess whether they should use the set hanging in the guest bath.

A stack of general interest magazines will be welcomed by a guest who wakes before the rest of the household.

Lay one or two extra blankets at the foot of the bed in case your guest needs a little more warmth in the night.

Another nice touch for your guest room is a bedside basket filled with tissues, an alarm clock, and a few simple snacks.

Don't have a guest room? A day bed, futon, sleeper sofa or inflatable bed in the family room or office can allow either room to serve as a temporary guest room.

CHAPTER XII

CLOSETS

Even the smallest closet can be outfitted with space saving racks for a small price. One handy item is a small $5.00 wire rack that you attach to the wall of your closet. It can be used to hold belts, ties or scarves.

Double the size of your closet by adding a second clothes rod below the top rod.

If you have a walk-in closet, hang an ironing board rack that holds both your iron and the board in the closet and it will be handy whenever you notice that a shirt you're putting on could use a quick touch up.

Keep two baskets or laundry hampers in your closet, one for lights and one for darks. As you undress, just drop your clothing in the appropriate basket and you'll never have to sort your dirty laundry again.

Hanging shoe bags hold more than shoes. Keep one in your entryway closet to hold gloves, small umbrellas and rolled up scarves. Use one in another spot to store small hand tools and dog grooming necessities. Hanging shoe bags can also store cleaning supplies, craft supplies or anything else that fits in those small pockets. You can buy inexpensive clear ones at a discount store or you can buy expensive decorator styles at the bed and bath stores.

Even if you do use a shoe bag or rack to store your shoes, don't throw away the shoeboxes they come in. Those little boxes are priceless organizers. They can be used as dividers in large drawers or they can be stacked on closet shelves to hide craft supplies or seldom worn accessories.

Minimize hanger marks on blouses and sweaters by hanging them inside out.

CHAPTER XIII

GARAGES

Whether you install a sophisticated wall system, a good old-fashioned pegboard or simple nails hammered into the walls, put those garage walls to good use and hang up everything possible.

You can hang up your tools, folding lawn furniture, hoses, extension cords and that horrible painting your Aunt Bertha gave you.

You can hang your bikes on hooks mounted on the walls or ceiling beams. If you have a little more money to invest, you can buy a pulley system that allows you to raise your bike to the ceiling without wrenching your back. These systems can be purchased at bicycle stores for around $50.00.

If you have one of those wire laundry racks that fits over the washer and dryer but you're not using it in the laundry room, put it to use in the garage by storing your trashcans under it instead of the washer and dryer.

Install an inexpensive paper towel rack in the garage. It will come in handy for family members who need to check their oil or tend to other chores in the garage.

Label a large box "spare parts." Any time you bring a new item into the house and it has unneeded pieces or replacement parts, (think odd-sized replacement light bulbs, for example) put them in your spare parts box. Anytime you need to fix anything, you'll know exactly where to find the parts you need.

CHAPTER XIV

CARS

Slide a shoebox between the front seats of your minivan or SUV to keep tissue boxes, hand wipes and CDs from rolling around on the floor.

Keep a cooler in your trunk or cargo area for your groceries and you won't have to worry about the ice cream melting in transit. If space is sometimes a problem in your trunk, buy a cooler that folds up when not in use.

For peace of mind, as well as for emergencies, always keep a flashlight and an emergency road kit in your car. A can of flat tire fixit and an emergency jump box might also save you some tense moments on the highway. Some jump boxes also have wonderful built-in spotlights.

Keep a supply of small trash bags in the car and you'll cut down on clutter rolling about.

Even if you prefer large umbrellas, keeping a small travel umbrella under your front seat may turn out to be a lifesaver (well, okay, a hairdo saver) if you happen to leave your large umbrella elsewhere.

Keep a little reading material or some catalogs in the car and time spent waiting in line at the bank or the drive-thru restaurant won't seem quite so irritating.

Keep an old blanket in the car all year round. It can keep backseat occupants warm and cozy on cold trips and it can come in handy for an impromptu picnic in the summer. An old pillow can also come in handy on a long drive.

Stash an old pair of sneakers in the car to change into if parking at the mall is bad or an unexpected rainstorm has you fretting about soaking your good high heel pumps.

Hand wipes seem like a no-brainer if you're traveling with children but you really need them for yourself, too. The next time you go to the gas pump or bank machine, look at the guy in line ahead of you. Do you know where his hands have been? Do you really want to touch the ATM buttons or the gas pump handle he just touched?

Instead of throwing your old phonebook in the trash when the new one comes, toss it under a seat in your car. If you have to phone your doctor to confirm your appointment or need to check to see if a business is open, the number will be right there handy when you need it. Also, many phonebooks have city maps in the front of the book and restaurant or store coupons in the back.

Why keep your fast food coupons in the kitchen drawer when you most often use them in the car? Put them in an envelope placed in your car's map pocket or glove compartment and you'll always have them when you need them – when you're out in the car.

Every time you stop to fill up with gas, empty the trash from your car into the container next to the pump.

Rather than hanging your bag chairs in the garage in the summer, stash them in the car and you'll always be ready to make yourself comfortable at outdoor parties and concerts.

Drop a drinking glass into your car drink holder to hold ink pens, nail files or cell phones.

CHAPTER XV

LAUNDRY

Keep a small jar for change next to your washer. It's amazing how fast the spare change that shows up in washer can add up. Use the money that you collect in that jar for a treat for the entire family, such as a movie or a special dinner.

Clean the dryer lint trap after every load you run.

Mount a towel bar in the laundry room to hang clothes as soon as you take them out of the dryer, before wrinkles have a chance to set in.

Every time you take a laundry basket or hamper to the laundry room, grab all of the empty hangers from your closet as you go so that they will be handy when that load comes out of the dryer.

Keep a pair of scissors in the laundry room to cut tags off of new clothing before you wash it.

Try to wash and dry one load of laundry every day and you'll cut down on the major pile-ups.

CHAPTER XVI

GROCERY SHOPPING

Use junk mail envelopes to write your shopping list on and then stash your coupons inside. To remind yourself that you have coupons for specific brands of some items on your list, underline that item on the list. While you're shopping you'll be reminded to choose the brand that you have a coupon for.

In order to prevent impulse shopping for junk food and impulse items, shop the perimeter of store first. All the basics you need, fresh fruits and vegetables, bread, milk and meat, are located on the outer aisles of the store. After you fill your cart with those necessities, only shop the aisles that contain items you truly need, such as canned items.

Don't assume discount stores will always have the lowest prices. You may find that the locally based grocery stores have better sales and will save you money over shopping at the big box stores. Most local stores also have a frequent customer reward program that will save you quite a bit on your weekly grocery bill.

Make copies of the sample grocery list in Chapter XXII. Take a copy of the list, check the items you need, make any additions of special items you need and you're ready to roll. Post a copy on the fridge and if at all possible, train your family members to check items needed on the list as they use the last one on hand.

When you get to the store, try to park next to the cart return. It's much easier to load your groceries in the car in this area and you'll be able to return your cart by taking just one or two steps.

Before making any large purchases, go to the product manufacturer or store website. Many websites offer substantial savings for customers who visit their website, often up to as much as 30% off of any purchase.

Don't put all of your frequent customer cards on the same key ring that holds your car key. Loading down that make it heavy enough to cause damage to your car's ignition over time. Grab an extra key ring and use it for all of the little shopping cards.

CHAPTER XVII

PAPERWORK & COMPUTER FILES

Email emergency back-up copies of your documents to yourself instead of saving them to disk. You can always open the entire document in a new file directly from that email because it is always out there on the email server.

You need an in-box. You can buy one from the office supply store or create one from a basket, the lid from a letterhead box or any old box that suits your needs. Put bills to be paid and letters to be answered in your in-box. Create a separate file or box for filing. Filing can wait but bills need to be taken care within a limited time. You'll save yourself time sorting out bills from junk mail if bills are the only items in your in-box.

Creating order in your computer files will save you a lot time. Do you tire of having to search through all of your daughter's homework and your husband's records to find that Christmas newsletter you were working on? Create separate computer files for different projects. If several people use the same computer, create one master file for each user and you'll never have to worry that another family member will inadvertently save over one of your files. Create one file named "Household" where you and your spouse keep all the financial records, home repair records, etc.

Create a file on your computer and call it the "Family Album," so that everyone in the household can look at or work with all the pictures stored there.

Speaking of pictures, when organizing your shots, get rid of the unflattering ones. Why keep any photos that don't make you and your family look your very best?

Order postage stamps on-line, buy them from your postal carrier, or get them from the ATM. Yes, the ATM. Check out the "other menus" option on the bank machine screen to see if your bank offers this service.

If you have a backlog of magazines you want to read, trying ripping out and saving individual articles instead of entire magazines. Stash them in your car to read while you're waiting on the kids or sitting in line at the bank.

When you burn down a candle, take a good look at the dish it came in. You may be able to repurpose it and use it to hold paper clips, rubber bands and other desktop necessities.

Store major appliance manuals in clear plastic storage bags tapped to side or back of the appliance.

Put your small kitchen appliance manuals in a binder with pockets and store it in the kitchen with cookbooks.

Don't have a filing cabinet? Plastic lidded bins make great airtight containers for your files. Buy as many as you need and stack them in a closet or the attic. Label them according to category, such as taxes, school papers, home improvement, etc.

Every December 31, create a tax envelope. Mark it with the year and put it wherever you sort your mail and pay your bills. As important tax documents arrive, slip them into the envelope and you'll be ready to roll at tax time.

You need only keep most documents seven years, which is the IRS standard. However, keep home improvement documents as long as you keep the house so that you have documentation of your long-term investment.

Throw away utility bills as soon as the next one comes in and you're sure that the new one is correct.

Shred ATM and grocery store receipts as soon as you balance your check book. Create a file or a box marked "shred" and shred things just once a month.

To cut down on clutter and to reduce risk of identity theft, have your credit card statements and bank statements emailed to you rather than sent through the postal service.

CHAPTER XVIII

TRAVEL

Travel can be as trying as a mini-move. After all, you have to pick up and move the things you need to get by. It can be a wonderful adventure or it can be a chore. Doing a few small tasks in advance will ensure that your trip will be a wonderful adventure.

The most important preparation you can do for your trip is to do a little advance research on the Internet.

If you're flying, check the airline's website just before you go. You can check on the latest packing restrictions, any flight changes and whether or not your flight is expected to leave on time. Most also allow you to "check in" on-line up to 24-hours in advance, even allowing you to print your boarding pass.

If you're traveling by car, go to the Mapquest, Rand McNally or Yahoo websites for directions, highway construction reports and even up-to-the-minute traffic reports.

Visit your hotel's website for information regarding gyms, pools and parking.

For short trips, use an old contact case to transport small dabs of make-up or medicines.

Save the plastic bags your newspaper comes in and use them to protect your shoes in your suitcase. They are also useful for covering your smaller umbrellas.

Put all of your cosmetics, shampoos, etc., in Ziploc bags to prevent them from leaking onto the clothing in your suitcase.

Always pack a lint roller for quick clean-ups.

If you like to shop when you travel, be sure to pack a folding bag for your purchases. If you really like to shop, pack the things you need for the trip in a medium sized bag, and then slide that bag into an extra large suitcase and you'll have an extra bag to bring home goodies from your travels.

If you're going on a business trip and need to have materials with you, such as P.R. materials or training manuals, ship them to your hotel in advance. Simply call your hotel or conference center and tell the staff there to expect the package for you. They should have it waiting for you upon your arrival.

If you're traveling by car with little ones and you aren't using the drive for an educational experience, travel at night or very early in the morning. They'll sleep most of the way.

If you happen to forget the portable video player, use your laptop for a video player to entertain the kids in the car or yourself in the hotel room.

Be sure to take some road snacks along with you. Fruit, chips, crackers and popcorn all work well. Orange slices are known to help ease motion sickness.

Use a three-ring binder with pockets to create a travel organizer. Include any necessary medical forms, directions and hotel confirmations. While traveling, you can put receipts in one of the pockets. Your binder will also come in handy for use as a travel diary.

Whatever you do, don't put all your money for the trip in one place. If someone steals your purse from the rest stop restroom, you could be in dire trouble. Mix up your money – put some in your pocket, some in your purse, some hidden in the car. If you are traveling with another adult, split the money between you.

Don't rely on just one bank card when you're traveling. Take some cash, your bank card, a credit card, if you have one, and the new version of traveler's checks, prepaid cash cards.

When packing, put whatever outfit you intend to wear the first day into your suitcase last. That way you won't have to dig for it. If you plan on sightseeing and taking a daypack with you, pack it and put it into your suitcase last, as well.

If you're leaving a pet at home with a pet sitter, be sure to leave some cash for emergency care.

When you return from your trip, stash an overnight bag with some travel essentials. If you're ever called away on a sudden family emergency, you'll be able to run out the door on a moment's notice.

When traveling by airline, be sure to mark your bags both inside and out. If you have them, use your business cards. In the alternative, mark your bags with your name and phone number. You don't want to put your address on your bags in case a local thief grabs your bag and figures out that your home will be unattended for a short time.

If you're using rolling luggage, put the heavy items in the back and bottom of your bag to prevent tipping.

Amusement parks seem to be a large part of many families' travel plans. Here are some tips that will help you make the most of your day in any theme park:

- Study the park's website. Most websites will provide everything you need to know in advance, such as hours, prices, restaurant choices and stroller availability.

- If you decide to try the restaurants at the park, be sure to find out if you need reservations. Some amusement park restaurants are booked up to three months in advance.

- Dress sensibly. An amusement park is not the place to dress up. Think about it. At the end of the day, you will be tired and sweaty, and you might possibly be covered in ice cream stains or other sticky substances you cannot identify. The most important thing you can do for your comfort is to wear sneakers or other comfortable shoes. You will be walking miles throughout the day and you will be standing in line. You will be stepping up and down into all kinds of rides. You may be sitting on the ground to watch a parade or the fireworks. You want everything you wear to be as comfortable as possible and totally washable.

- Get to the park as early in the day as possible. Most amusement park parking lots open as early as an hour before the park does. This allows you to get in, get a good spot and possibly even buy your tickets before the park actually opens.

- Be prepared to go through security checkpoints before entering the park. Limit what you carry with you to essentials only. Have your bags unzipped or unbuttoned and ready for security to poke through when your turn comes.

- Try to get your tickets before you go. Some offer advance purchase of tickets on-line or at certain retail shops. If you don't buy your tickets in advance, when you get to the park, look for ticket vending machines. They work just like a bank machine and can save you from having to wait in line for up to as much as an hour.

- Studies have shown the when most people enter an amusement park, they turn to the right. Your plan is to turn left. The rides to the left of the park will be the least crowded at the beginning of the day. You'll be working in the opposite direction from most of the crowd, so you'll be able to avoid the long lines at least for a while.

- Read the park's website or brochure to see if they have a fast ticket option for the most popular rides. By getting a fast ticket to the main events, you'll be allowed to bypass the long lines and walk right onto the best rides.

- While amusement parks generally don't allow you to take food into the park, most do provide picnic areas in the parking area. Pack a cooler and leave it in the car. Get a pass out at lunchtime, have a restful picnic in the shade and then return to the park to enjoy the rest of your day. You'll avoid the long lines (and high prices) of the park's restaurants. Bonus – if you take a blanket to spread out on the ground, you and/or the kids can take a short nap and awake fully ready to endure the rest of the day.

- Take frequent drink and potty breaks. The restroom lines can be long, so plan to make pit stops at frequent intervals to avoid any frantic potty dances in long lines.

- Don't sugar up the kids. You don't want them any more wired than they will already be and you definitely don't want to deal with an emotional crash when the sugar wears off.
- If you really don't care to sit and watch the parades, take advantage of those times to hit the big attractions. With most of the crowd parked in front of the main show, you may be able to walk right onto the best rides in the park.
- To make sure you have everything you need but aren't stuck carrying a tote or purse, take a daypack with the basics: Water bottles, hand sanitizer, camera, tissues, paper napkins, sunscreen, sunglasses, sun visors, granola bars, etc.
- If you make purchases at one of the many shops scattered throughout the park, have the shop send the purchase to the visitor center at the front of the park. You'll be able to pick up your package as you leave and won't have to lug it around with you all day.
- Rent a locker at the amusement park entrance and stash jackets in there until you need them.
- If you have little ones, consider renting the park stroller instead of taking your own. They are inexpensive and specifically made to maneuver through the park. Plus, you won't have to worry about something unfortunate happening to your expensive stroller.

CHAPTER XIX

HOLIDAYS

The holidays seem to be the center of American life. Many of us plan our holidays all year long, even if it is only in our heads. Indeed, if you can spread the work over the course of the year, not only will you have more time to actually enjoy the holidays when they come, but it will also be less of a blow to your budget.

Buy your gift wrap and small gifts from the kids during their early fall school fundraising sales.

Before all the holiday madness begins, be sure to stock up on basics such baking goods, paper goods, wrapping paper, tape and assorted batteries. If you wear department store cosmetics, check your stash and make sure you have all you need to get through the holidays. You really don't want to have to fight the mall crowds just because you ran out of your favorite eyeliner at an inconvenient time.

Shop on-line wherever possible. You'll have the luxury of shopping from the comfort of your own home, plus you won't have the hassles of driving to the mall, searching for a parking place and lugging heavy packages back to the car. The gifts you order on-line can be sent to you or directly to the recipient. Most on-line retailers even offer gift wrapping.

If you prefer to go to the store, try to go during off-peak hours. Very early in the morning and late in the evening are particularly good times for avoiding crowds. If you're already out at a Christmas party during the evening and know that you have to run to one of the big box stores in the next day or so, just stop on your way home. The store crowds drop dramatically after 9:00 p.m.

To streamline your shopping, consider a gift theme. Perhaps you would like to give everyone books this year. One stop at the bookstore and you'll be done.

Wineries are a great place to buy gifts and while busy during the holidays, are much less crowded than the malls. Most offer much more than wine. Many wineries also sell gourmet foods, candles, home accessories and picnic baskets.

One of the best places to get last minute gifts is Cracker Barrel. You can have breakfast there and then on your way out pick up toys, candles, clothing, books and countless other fun gifts for everyone on your list.

Set up a gift wrap center, even if your center is just a cardboard box. Include scissors, tape, wrap, tags, etc., so that you never have to go searching for those items when you're wrapping a gift. Use the same box year after year and keep it stocked at all times. If you live in a two story house, consider keeping one on each floor so that if the recipient is upstairs, you can wrap his/her gift downstairs and vice versa.

Do your cards while you're relaxing in front of a good Christmas movie or football game. Put the kids to work affixing stamps and licking those envelopes. Even husbands can help out with addressing envelopes, particularly if you keep your list on the computer and print out the addresses on peel and stick labels.

Your home can be beautifully decorated without spending a lot of time or money. Try some of these quick and easy ideas:

- Tie red and green ribbon on everything that doesn't move.
- Drape tinsel from light fixtures and stair rails.
- Top tables with red & green candles. Place them on or in front of mirrors to double the glow.
- String popcorn to make garland for the tree.
- Have the kids make red & green construction paper chains to drape over mantels and the Christmas tree.
- Fill glass bowls with Christmas balls.
- Display the holiday cards you receive on top of your entertainment center and bookcases.
- Top entertainment centers, bookcases and cabinets with poinsettias.

- Create special collages with holiday pictures taken over the years and prop them on benches and shelves.
- Raid the kids' rooms for teddy bears (currently unused, of course), dress them in red ribbons, put small wrapped gifts in their arms and arrange them on small bench or in a wagon.

Keep emergency gifts on hand for unexpected visitors such as your son's new girlfriend. Candles, books, games, wines, candy, picture frames, one-size-fits-all gloves and scarves are all welcome gifts for just about everyone. Gift cards for major retailers or restaurants work well also.

Keep a gift card in your purse and if a friend surprises you with a gift over lunch, you can whip out the gift card for her. The bonus is that if you don't need to give it as a gift over the holidays, you can spend it yourself later.

Are you on a limited income or have difficulty getting out shopping? Consider giving some of the family heirlooms to your kids and grandkids. Cookbooks, albums and dishware would all be welcome gifts. Not only will you have given them something they cherish, but you'll have the personal joy of seeing them enjoy your things during your lifetime.

Does giving cash or a gift card seem impersonal to you? It's all in the presentation. Try putting the cash or card into a special container such as a picture frame, piggy bank, wallet or purse.

Use slice and bake cookie dough instead of starting from scratch. Most kids are more interested in decorating than baking anyway.

Stocking stuffers can sometimes cost more than regular gifts. To save money on stocking stuffers, shop the Dollar Store or the dollar aisle at Target for fun, inexpensive gifts that everyone will enjoy. For kids, buy party favors as stocking fillers.

Give homemade gift certificates for services that only you can provide – think babysitting, cooking, housecleaning, painting, lawn care and dog walking. Use your computer's word processing program to create professional looking certificates.

For your grown children, give them albums filled with pictures of their childhood.

Create a family history album for your parents and your children. Include a family tree and all of the best family stories that you can recall.

Create a family cookbook to give all the members of your family. Fill it with the old family favorites and include pictures and stories related to each recipe.

Consider giving "serial" gifts. You may not be able to afford an entire set of fine dishes or CDs all at one time, but you may be able to buy one piece for a loved one every year. You'll be able to complete the collection over time without breaking your budget.

Make a special effort at the end of every October to plan your holiday calendar. Check your church and school websites for important dates, as well as your work calendar. Don't forget to schedule in time for your holiday tasks such as addressing cards, shopping, gift wrapping, baking and entertaining.

CHAPTER XX

ENTERTAINING

Entertaining can be intimidating if you don't do it often. Once you've mastered the art of entertainment, it can prove to be one of the great joys in life. What could be better than sharing a relaxing evening in your home with friends and family? Below are some tips that will help you master the art.

Once you've decided upon a date and the guests for your party, send the invitations. Invitations should be sent two weeks before the event. You can call, send old-fashioned printed invitations by snail mail or send email invitations but be sure to send a map to your home along with the invitations. Once you create the map, save it on your computer for future use.

Plan your menu so that you don't spend the entire party either in the kitchen or jumping up to serve everyone. Most home parties wind up in the kitchen anyway, so you might as well embrace that fact and make it the center of the party.

These days, most people prefer casual parties where big pots of chili, salads and pizzas are served buffet style. Clean off your kitchen counters and use them as buffet serving areas. You need not have fancy serving pieces for this type of buffet. Just make the most of what you already have, including the kitchen sink. Fill that sink with ice to keep canned sodas chilled.

If you would rather use an ice bucket but don't have one, a soup tureen can serve as a nice substitute. Most tureens come with ladles that work well for scooping ice.

There's no need to buy a food warmer. Keep soup or chili warm by keeping them right on the stove in your nicest pans. Crock pots work well for this also.

These days, most family dining tables only seat six to eight people. If you want to host more people than that, set up extra tables. You may find that a card table butts up nicely to your dinning room table and that once covered with a tablecloth, no one will be the wiser.

If your dining room is too small for your party, consider setting up tables in the living room, family room or basement. If weather permits, move your party to the patio or deck.

If coat storage is an issue, putting guests' coats on the bed is still a time-honored tradition. If you have a closet by the front door, consider making room for the guest coats in there by moving everything out of there and onto a bed just for the duration of the party.

The most important thing you can do to ensure your guests' comfort is to make sure your powder room has a fresh roll of toilet paper, fresh towels, plenty of soap and a trash can.

If you have pets, for their comfort and the comfort of your guests, consider sending them to friend's house for the duration of the party.

If you have sports equipment or other large items cluttering your entertainment space, stash them in the trunk of your car for the time being.

CHAPTER XXI

HOUSEHOLD MOVES

Nothing turns our lives upside down as thoroughly as a household move. At the same time, nothing creates as much opportunity to become organized as a move does. During a move, you literally handle each and every one of your belongings, so take the opportunity to weed through things and get them in order.

The moment you first know that you will be moving, start going through your belongings and get rid of everything you don't need or want. There is no better time than a move to get this task done. Start with the closets and the drawers, sorting out everything you haven't used in the last year. Either sell it at a garage sale or cart if off to Goodwill.

Create a file or binder strictly for the move. Include your to do lists, receipts, estimates, utility information, closing information, etc.

Use a color coding system. Mark each box with colored tape or colored dots on the boxes. Use a different color for each room. Create a legend showing that boxes with red markings go in the kitchen, blue in the bedroom, etc. When you get to the new house, put a dot or piece of the tape on the door jam to each room and you'll know at a glance which boxes go in which room.

Your most important box will be your survival box. On moving day, guard this one with your life. Make sure it rides in the car with you and that you know exactly where it is at all times. What to put in this box? All the things that you absolutely cannot live without: Toilet paper, soap, tissues, picnic supplies, paper towels, bedding, medicines, light bulbs and anything else you might need right away.

Change your mailing address for the grand cost of $1.00 at usps.com. You'll also find helpful moving tips there. An added bonus is that after you complete your address change on-line, you'll receive generous coupons for services and products that anyone moving could use.

You don't need to fold and pack hanging clothes. Simply cover them with large trash bags in which you have poked a hole for the hangers.

A move is also a good time to have your comforters dry cleaned. Take your comforter to the dry cleaner a day or two before you move and it should be ready to pick up on moving day.

Don't box your books. Use twine to bind them together in small stacks. You'll be able to pick them up by the twine.

Wrap breakables in your tea towels, bath towels and beach towels.

Don't pack the boxes too full. It's easier to lug several small boxes rather than just a few boxes that are too heavy for one person to lift.

When loading the truck (or supervising moving men) make sure that the things you want to go into the new home first are the last things that are put onto the truck. This is especially important for high need items like baby beds or your kitchen table and chairs.

When you get to the new house, be sure to take a few moments to flip through your new phone book or neighborhood welcome packet. You'll find invaluable information and coupons there.

When moving to a new city, the library can be a wonderful source of information. In addition to public bulletin boards with postings regarding community events, many libraries offer wonderful educational programs, often for free or at a very low price. You'll also find great magazines and books there that will guide you in decorating your new home.

CHAPTER XXII

LISTS

Here are some basic lists that can make your life easier. Please feel free to take this book to a copy machine and make as many copies of these lists as you need. I've left some blank lines at the end of each page so you can customize each list to suit your lifestyle.

GROCERY SHOPPING

Apples	Ketchup	Spaghetti Sauce
Bananas	Lettuce	Spices
Beans	Marshmallows	Sugar
Beef	Mayonnaise	Syrup
Bread	Milk	Tea
Buns	Mustard	Toilet Paper
Butter	Onions	Tomatoes
Cake Mix	Oranges	Vinegar
Carrots	Pancake Mix	_____
Cereal	Paper Napkins	_____
Cheese	Paper Towels	_____
Chicken	Pasta	_____
Cocoa	Peas	_____
Coffee	Pepper	_____
Creamer	Pet Food	_____
Cooking Oil	Pizza	_____
Crackers	Popcorn	_____
Cream	Pork	_____
Cucumbers	Potatoes	_____
Eggs	Pudding	_____
Fish	Radishes	_____
Flour	Rice	_____
Frosting	Salt	_____
Green Beans	Snack Cheese	_____
Ice Cream	Soda	_____
Instant Potatoes	Soups	_____
Juice	Sour Cream	

HOLIDAY GIFT LIST

Name _____
Gift _____
Color _____ Size _____
Price _____ Store _____

Name _____
Gift _____
Color _____ Size _____
Price _____ Store _____

Name _____
Gift _____
Color _____ Size _____
Price _____ Store _____

Name _____
Gift _____
Color _____ Size _____
Price _____ Store _____

Name _____
Gift _____
Color _____ Size _____
Price _____ Store _____

CHRISTMAS CARD REGISTER

Name _____
Address _____
_____

Name _____
Address _____
_____

Name _____
Address _____
_____

Name _____
Address _____
_____

Name _____
Address _____
_____

Name _____
Address _____
_____

Name _____
Address _____
_____

Name _____
Address _____
_____

Name _____
Address _____
_____

Name _____
Address _____
_____

Name _____
Address _____
_____

Name _____
Address _____
_____

Name _____
Address _____
_____

Name _____
Address _____
_____

Name _____
Address _____
_____

Name _____
Address _____
_____

Name _____
Address _____
_____

Name _____
Address _____
_____

Name _____
Address _____
_____

Name _____
Address _____
_____

Name _____
Address _____
_____

TRAVEL PACKING LIST

Bathing Suit	Medicines	Umbrella
Beach Shoes	Pajamas	Underwear for ___ Days
Camera & Spare Batteries	Pants/Skirts for ___ Days	_____
Cell Phone	Pillows	_____
Cell Phone Charger	Plastic Bags for Shoes	_____
Cosmetics	Robe	_____
Directions and Maps	Sewing Kit	_____
Emergency Road Kit	Shirts for ___ Days	_____
First-Aid Kit	Snacks	_____
Games	Socks/Hosiery for ___ Days	_____
Hair Dryer	Spare Shoes	_____
Hand Wipes	Sunglasses or Sunhat	_____
Jacket	Trash Bags	_____
Make-Up Mirror	Travel Binder	

BEFORE LEAVING HOME

_____ Have your mail stopped. Go to the postal service website at usps.com to have this done.

_____ Have your newspaper put on vacation hold. Most publishers will either credit your account or donate the unused papers to charity.

_____ Make arrangements for pet/plant care. Leave instructions, vet name & phone number.

_____ If traveling by car, have it serviced before you hit the road.

_____ Set water heater to vacation setting.

_____ Unplug small appliances, such as video players, clock radios and coffee makers.

_____ Put household lights on a timer.

_____ Set out the clothes you will wear to work the first day back.

_____ Put the trash out for collection or arrange for a neighbor to do it.

_____ Clean out the refrigerator.

_____ Wash the last dishes you use before leaving.

HELPFUL WEBSITES

BEST FOR HOUSEHOLD ITEMS, CLOTHING AND GIFTS:

- Amazon.com
- Harryanddavid.com
- Swisscolony.com
- Atasteofindiana.com
- Walmart.com
- Target.com
- Lillianvernon.com
- Crateandbarrel.com
- Sears.com
- Potterybarn.com
- Plowhearth.com
- Llbean.com

BEST FOR DECORATING IDEAS:

- Bhg.com
- HGTV.com
- Lowes.com
- Homedepot.com
- Womansday.com
- Familycircle.com
- Marthastewart.com

BEST FOR COOKING:

- Bettycrocker.com
- Butterball.com
- Kraft.com
- Jello.com

BEST FOR ORGANIZING IDEAS:

- Organizerdee.tripod.com
- Lifeorganizers.com
- ContainerStore.com
- Realsimple.com
- Homedepot.com
- Stacksandstacks.com
- Calclosets.com
- Ikea-usa.com
- Westelm.com
- Organize.com

www.ingramcontent.com/pod-product-compliance
Lightning Source LLC
Chambersburg PA
CBHW031416040426
42444CB00005B/600